Earth Action
©Della Burford 2021
Azatlan Publishing
Co-Author Dale Bertrand
Editing - Jacquie Howardson

Original book Magical Earth Secrets
Western Canada Wilderness Commitee
Original Environmental Activity Guide
Azatlan Publishing

Re-edit of Guide
with Della at the Space Camp 2022 and 2023
of the Buckminster Fuller Institute
Many helped and collaborated
Special thanks to Faith Flanigan
also Roxi Shohanidee & Bliss Alberts
Design Science Studio
Please see Thank you page
ISBN 978-1-927825-17-4

Dedication:

*To Buckminster Fuller who
has been an inspiration to many.
He believed we must have spontaneous
cooperation without any damage
to the environment
and without disadvantage to anyone.
For his imaginative inventions,
and respecting and using nature as an
honored teacher.
His work became for humanity
when realizing
he was part of the universe.
May his work encourage others*

to make their work for humanity and all living things.

Bucky Quotes:

*"We live on a spaceship. The trouble is an operating manual
didn't come with it."
"We are not going to be able to operate our Spaceship Earth
successfully nor for much
longer unless we see it as a whole spaceship and
our fate as common. It has to be
everybody or nobody."
"children want to understand the universe,
and we teach them their ABC's"*

*(To honor "Bucky" we have included
6 Inventions & 6 Activities in the "Earth Action" book)*

Index for "Earth Action"

Eagle Child - Rainbow Wings

THE MAGICAL EARTH SECRETS story in a nutshell.

Once upon a time there was an eagle child called Rainbow Wing. eagle was not and ordinary child but a mythical, imaginary creature that had an eagle's head and a child's feet and legs.

We did not know if this was a boy or girl, we just know it was part magical child and could talk. Rainbow Wings lived in two place and had two families. Part of the time it lived in the mountain with eagle brother and sister, and the rest in the city with human brothers and sisters.

One hot day Rainbow Wings felt thirsty and went for a drink in the lake. But the water was not clean and Rainbow Wings felt dizzy and sick. The air was also polluted.

Rainbow Wings felt scared and sad. The beautiful colors on were faded and gone and said, "I have lost my power to fly. How can I get my power back?

Rainbow Wings knew of a place nearby with a Wise One and decided to go for help. The Wise One said, "To get you power and magic colors you must go and meet the little people of the four directions. You must go east, then south, then west and north. You must travel through the four seasons. The little people have some secret words called the "Magical Earth Secrets" to get your strength again."
(The story continues in each section of this guide).

Earth Seed said:
"Here's the secret words:
I and the Earth are one.
I love the Earth.
I will take care
of the Earth."
Eagle Child said,
"The red on my wings
is brighter
and brighter."

The Seasons Wheel

The Season Wheel turns. Spring eggs become chicks. Summer flowers blossom. Fall leaves turn colors and fall. In winter the bear takes a rest and sleeps and dreams. A flower dies but its seeds go back in the earth. Spring seeds can sprout again. The Season Wheel turns.

What is the best time to rest, start something new and flower?

The Waste-Not Wheel

The energy to keep the Waste -Not Wheel turning over and over again is coming from the Sun, water, wind. Conserve nature's gifts that provide us with energy to live the life we want to live. When we throw garbage away we are throwing away valuable resources. Recyle, reduce, and upcycle. Conserve and compost. Let the Waste-Not Wheel turn.

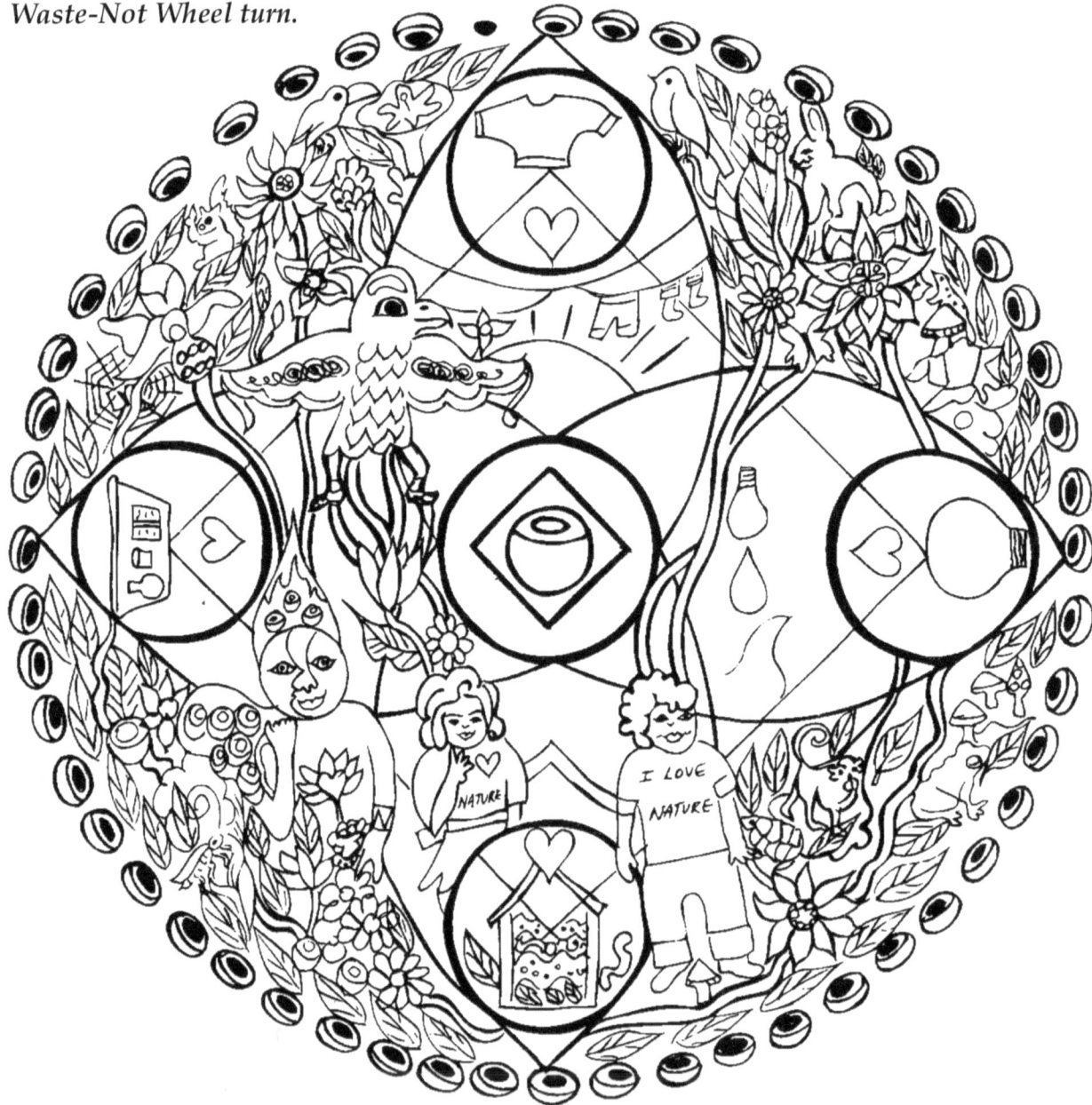

Why is recycling, reducing and upcycling important?

"Love the Trees" Poster

One of Earth Seeds jobs is planting trees. Study the various kinds of trees, their shapes, and the kind of leaves they have and where they grow. Think of your favourite trees and do drawings of them. Biodiversity with many different types of plants is best in a garden . The trees help give off oxygen from their leaves. They also help keep the land cool in the summer, they collect and recycle water, some provide fruit and and nuts and homes for the animals. They are beautiful.

"Endangered Animal" Poster

Earth Seed takes care of the endangered animals. When each year there are fewer and fewer of an animal or plant we call them endangered. There are many animals and plants that are endangered and threatened. Some that are well known are the Giant Panda, Mountain Gorilla, Tiger, Orangutan, Sea Turtles, Grizzly Bear to name just a few. There are probably some in the area where you live so look these up . Some needing protection in Canada are the Killer Whales, Boreal Woodland Caribous, Sage Grouses, Mountain Caribous, Spotted Owls & Wild Salmon. Draw picture of animals in your area that need protection. Think of ways to make sure the threatened animals are protected and all living things. Let's not forget the insects too like the Bee. Make a poster to share your concern.

Do Upcycled Art!

Earth Seed likes to recycle and reduce waste. It is important to recycle as much as we can so we do not have to use the energy to make it again. We can save water, materials, electricity, trees, when we do not throw things away. Use organic materials and not plastics. We can also think of upcycling something and using it again in a new way. Make some Upcycled Art.

Earth Seed's Things to Do:

1. Plant a tree, 2. Plant a garden. 3. Help threatened animals in your area. Protect animals homes 5. Use alternatives to plastics.
6. Build a bird house. 7 Separate and store items to be recycled. 8. Take your old items to a charity. 9. Have garage sales. 10. Have or visit a Bee hive.

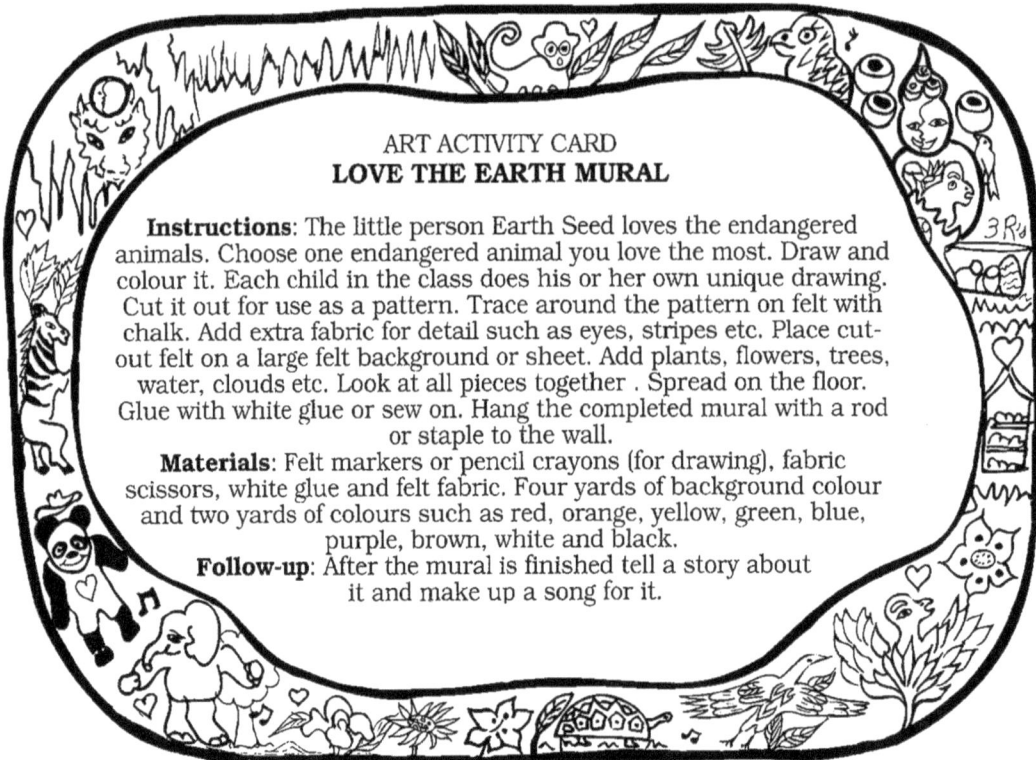

ART ACTIVITY CARD
LOVE THE EARTH MURAL

Instructions: The little person Earth Seed loves the endangered animals. Choose one endangered animal you love the most. Draw and colour it. Each child in the class does his or her own unique drawing. Cut it out for use as a pattern. Trace around the pattern on felt with chalk. Add extra fabric for detail such as eyes, stripes etc. Place cut-out felt on a large felt background or sheet. Add plants, flowers, trees, water, clouds etc. Look at all pieces together . Spread on the floor. Glue with white glue or sew on. Hang the completed mural with a rod or staple to the wall.

Materials: Felt markers or pencil crayons (for drawing), fabric scissors, white glue and felt fabric. Four yards of background colour and two yards of colours such as red, orange, yellow, green, blue, purple, brown, white and black.

Follow-up: After the mural is finished tell a story about it and make up a song for it.

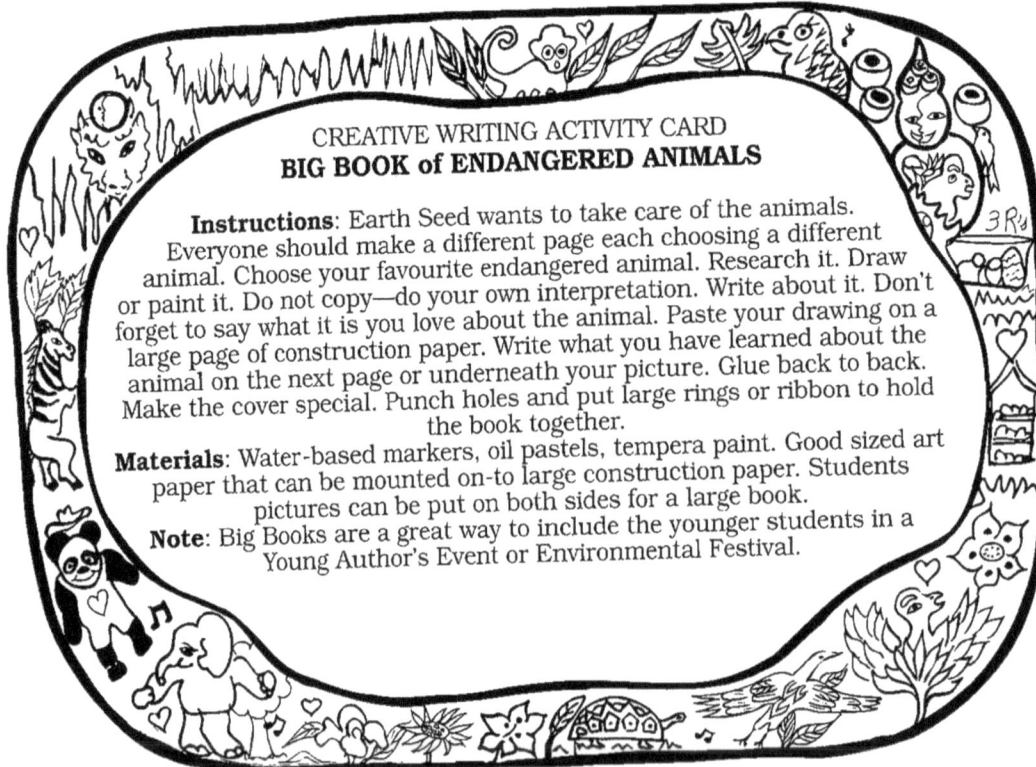

CREATIVE WRITING ACTIVITY CARD
BIG BOOK of ENDANGERED ANIMALS

Instructions: Earth Seed wants to take care of the animals. Everyone should make a different page each choosing a different animal. Choose your favourite endangered animal. Research it. Draw or paint it. Do not copy—do your own interpretation. Write about it. Don't forget to say what it is you love about the animal. Paste your drawing on a large page of construction paper. Write what you have learned about the animal on the next page or underneath your picture. Glue back to back. Make the cover special. Punch holes and put large rings or ribbon to hold the book together.

Materials: Water-based markers, oil pastels, tempera paint. Good sized art paper that can be mounted on-to large construction paper. Students pictures can be put on both sides for a large book.

Note: Big Books are a great way to include the younger students in a Young Author's Event or Environmental Festival.

What is regenerative farming ???

As described by **Earthday.org**

 https://www.earthday.org/campaign/regenerative-agriculture/

"American agriculture faces potentially devastating challenges. As a result of overfarming, development and other factors, soil capacity is dramatically declining, with some experts predicting fewer than 60 harvests remaining. The United States is losing soil 10 times faster than it's replenished. Ownership of large-scale farms — where most of the food and agricultural pollution comes from — is increasingly concentrated in the hands of industrial or foreign producers who tend to value short-term profits over the long-term health of our land and people.

Regenerative farming, however, offers solutions to transform farmers into **environmental and societal heroes.** It promotes the **health of degraded soils by restoring their organic carbon**. Regenerative agriculture sequesters atmospheric carbon dioxide, reversing industrial agriculture's contributions to climate change. Regenerative practices such as **no till farming and cover cropping are reducing erosion and water pollution, and in turn, producing healthier soils."**

Buckminster Fuller

Buckminster Fuller was an inventor, architect, mathematician, futurist and author. He is best known for the geodesic dome.

After the tragic death of his four year old daughter, and with mounting debts from a business failure, at the age of 32 Buckminster Fuller wondered if he should end his life. To his surprise he had a mystical experience and was reminded he belonged to the universe. He decided to make his life an experiment. He would be Guninea pig "B" and he would set out to discover what, if anything, a man of average means could do that would benefit humanity as a whole, with no one left out. The result of his life long experiment were designs and inventions unlike anything anyone has ever seen before. By the end of his life Bucky had 28 patents, for his designs and inventions, as well as being the author of 30 books which he shared world-wide. He was known as "Bucky, the planet's friendly genius".

Bucky popularized the term, Spaceship Earth to emphasize that like a spaceship the earth is traveling at enormous speeds, and that we are all crew members on Spaceship Earth. We need to work together to take care of our small spaceship and protect its resources.

There are now 300,000 geodesic domes around the world. The photo below was taken at the Science Center in Vancouver, Canada.

Dymaxion House

Buckminster Fuller designed a round house which combined the words dynamic, maximum and tension to arrive at Dymaxion. He saw shortcomings in the existing homebuilding techniques and addressed them in his invention. They used resources efficiently and he intended them to be suitable to any environment. He came up with his inventions by looking at nature's designs. The geometric design was stronger than routine structures. He reduced water use and had an alternative shower called a 'fogger'. They were easy to assemble and were portable and could be shipped easily. It used energy that was 'off the grid'. This design had exciting new ideas.

installed in Henry Ford Museum - photo by rmherman @ English wikipedia 18 April 2005 C.C.O. 1.0.

Your Dymaxion House

Instructions:

Design the interior of a Dymaxion house. This house is a circular house designed by Bucky. Find a photo of something you love in nature, it might be a flower you love or your favourite animal – it can live on the ground, trees, water, mountains or in the air. Look at the colors, shapes and textures of it and its surrounding. Use these colors, shapes and textures in choosing furniture, flooring, colors and accessories for your Dymaxion house. Draw the circular plan of your living room and/or bedroom as two circles. Place the furniture inside as shapes. Beside this put photos of what you see from the windows, a mural, types of furniture, colors and accessories. Another follow up suggested by an architect would be to design a house of another shape from nature e.g. shell, flower etc.

Materials: paper, Bristol board, scissors, glue, furniture photos, colors and accessories, found objects for texture, photos for view or mural

"When we Ask Nature, first we quiet our human cleverness.
Then we ask, and then we listen.
The answer is the echo that bounces off of the land herself.
With the solution in hand, we always end the circle by saying thank you."
—Janine Benyus

Ask Nature a Question??????

This beautiful quote is from Janine Beynus from the Biomimicy Institute. She has inspired and developed with a team of people a program to teach us about listening and being inspired by nature. Look at the website https://asknature.org . Here you can be an explorer and see many examples of how nature can teach us to deal with everyday questions and solve probems in a regenerative way. There is even a section for different age groups so it is something to enjoyed by all ages. Think of a question to ask nature. Check out the AskNature website:
https://asknature.org/educators/

Sweetwater whispered
the secret words:
"I and the water are one.
I love the water.
I will take care
of the water."
The Eagle Child
saw as well as red
a beautiful orange
color was on its wings.
Imagine the orange!

The Water Cycle Wheel

The Water Cycle turns. The sun heats the water. Some of the liquid water gains enough energy to change into water vapour. The water vapour rises, cools and becomes clouds. The water vapour in the clouds becomes liquid and sometimes freezes to become snow and hail. The Sun heats the water. The Water Wheel turns.

Is the water and air connected?

The Food Chain Wheel

The Food Chain Wheel turns. The bald eagles eats salmon The salmon eat herring. The herring eat zooplankton. The zooplankton eat phytoplankton. The sun's energy keeps the phytoplankton - the algaie green. The green algae absorbs and uses the sun's energy to make food. The sun brings forth a new day. The Food Wheel turns.

How are we connected to each other? Why is the sun & water important to all living things?

"Love the Water" Poster

One of Sweet Water's jobs is to take care of the water and make sure the animals and living things are safe in the water. Sweetwater knows the water covers 70% of the earth and we must take care of it. Taking care of the ocean and water in rivers and streams is crucial. Sweetwater wants our help to keep the water clean. To do this we have to know how it is polluted. Pollution happens when unwanted and harmful things get into the pure and clean water. Pollution is bad for all living things. One thing to do is to make sure no garbage goes in the water. Make a 'Love the Water' Poster.

"No Hazardous Wastes" Poster

Make sure you do not put any hazardous wastes down the drain of the sink like bleaches, paint thinners, and any chemicals. Use environmentally friendly products instead of chemicals. Baking soda and warm water is a good general cleaner.

"No Acid Rain" Poster

When water vapors mix with gases from factories, or with car exhausts, the water vapor dissolves and become acidic. It is called Acid Rain. If you see waste coming from the chimneys of factories write them and ask if they can take precautions to make sure wastes do not go in the air.

In the Water Cycle we see that when water vapor become clouds it then comes down to the water again. Unwanted chemicals in the water causes problems for plants growth which is food. Fish that are exposed sometimes cannot get oxygen in their blood and may not be able to lay eggs. When pollution happens the food chain can be broken.

Sweetwater suggests Things to Do:

1. Love the living things that live in the water 2. Use cars less – ride a bike if you can or walk or share a ride. 3. Pick up garbage if you see it thrown in the water. 4. Be careful what you throw down the drain. 4. Try alternative energy sources. 5. Write to a factory if you see they are polluting. 6. Show that you love and will take care of the water.

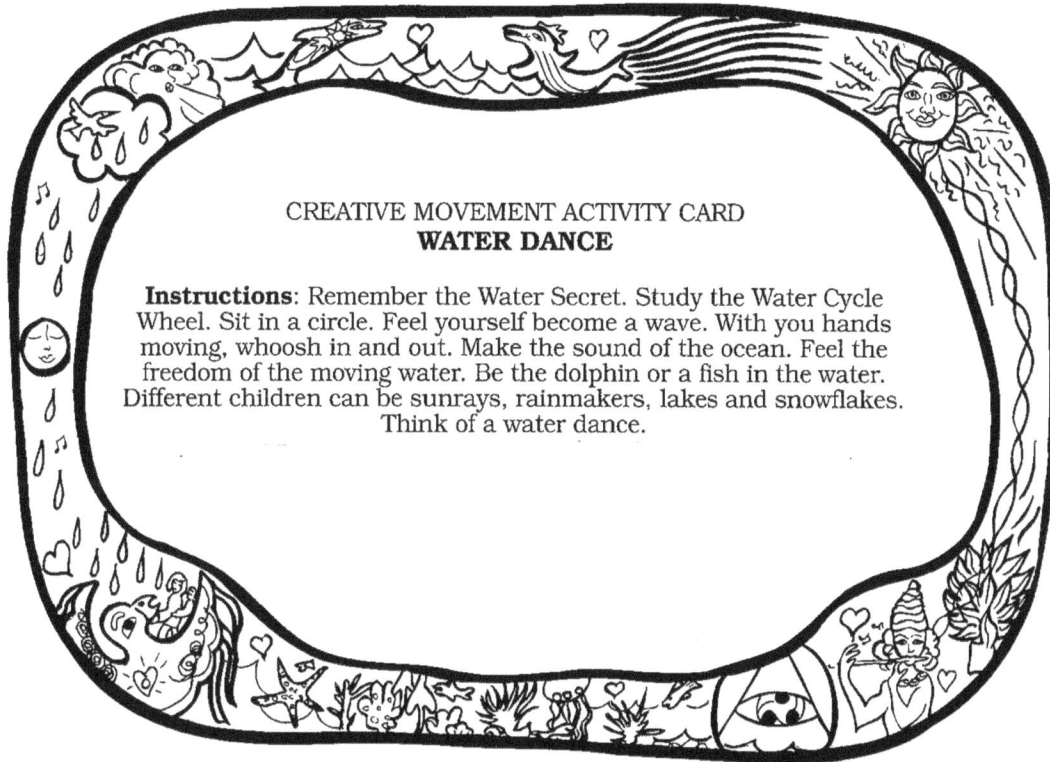

CREATIVE MOVEMENT ACTIVITY CARD
WATER DANCE

Instructions: Remember the Water Secret. Study the Water Cycle Wheel. Sit in a circle. Feel yourself become a wave. With you hands moving, whoosh in and out. Make the sound of the ocean. Feel the freedom of the moving water. Be the dolphin or a fish in the water. Different children can be sunrays, rainmakers, lakes and snowflakes. Think of a water dance.

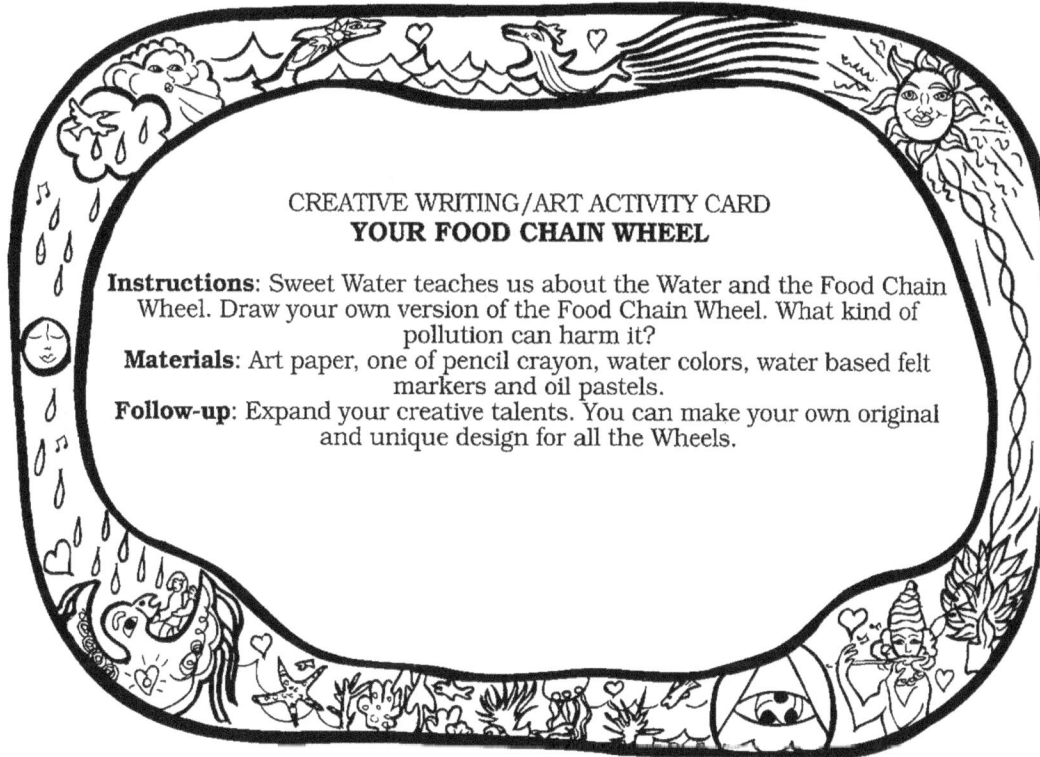

CREATIVE WRITING/ART ACTIVITY CARD
YOUR FOOD CHAIN WHEEL

Instructions: Sweet Water teaches us about the Water and the Food Chain Wheel. Draw your own version of the Food Chain Wheel. What kind of pollution can harm it?
Materials: Art paper, one of pencil crayon, water colors, water based felt markers and oil pastels.
Follow-up: Expand your creative talents. You can make your own original and unique design for all the Wheels.

Fly's Eye Dome

This dome structure was designed by Buckminster Fuller in 1965. He was designing with the idea of creating an affordable and portable home of the future. The name he has called it is the Fly Eye Dome as it has a structure like the eye of a fly when looked at under magnification. It has openings in which solar panels could be used. Also these openings could be a system for water collection.

In looking at Biomimicy we see many examples of inspiration from nature in solving probems and designing. There is a fascinating website on some of these inspirations. https://asknature.org/ around the work of Janine Benyus.

50 foot prototype Crystal Bridge Museum of American Art author : wmpearl Wikepedia Commons

What is Marine Permaculture? - Climate Foundation

https://climatefoundation.org - When I (Della) was in the second Space Camp of the Buckminster Fuller Institute Faith Flanigan arranged for Brian Von Herzen to come to speak to us. Here is a little about Brian and a description of Marine Permaculture.

Brian Von Herzen Ph.D. is the founder and executive director of the Climate Foundation, which upholds the vision and the mission to regenerate life in the ocean using Marine Permaculture technology. As Executive Director, Brian leads Climate Foundation's large-scale seaweed mariculture programs to develop sustainable food, feed and fertilizer value chains, provide ecosystem life support, and sustain blue carbon sinks.

"Marine Permaculture uses marine solar and wave-driven pumps in the ocean to restore natural upwelling and primary production to grow seaweed ecosystems. Seaweeds fix significant amounts of carbon and have multiple uses including food, feed, fuel, bio stimulants, and fertilizer. After sustainable harvesting, residual seaweed can be sunk to the bottom of the ocean sequestering carbon for centuries, facilitating drawdown of carbon from the atmosphere with extended Sea Forestation. Once deployed at scale Marine Permaculture can regenerate life in seas and soils and restore a healthy climate while building."

Three Goals: **FOOD SECURITY** – to provide enough food for human and other species. We provide for millions.

CARBON BALANCE - To find deploy carbon balancing systems that mimic natures once used ways.

ECOSYSTEM SURVIVAL – there is 8.7 million species losing their habitat – we provide a safe haven.

Sun Ray told
his powerful secret words:
"I and the sun are one.
I love the sun.
The sun takes care
of me."A bright
yellow color grew
on Eagle Child's
wings. Imagine
the yellow!

THE LIGHT WHEEL

The Light Wheel turns. Plants make their own food. The Sun makes leave green. Chlorophyll captures the Sun's energy.   Plants produce food for animals, birds, insects and humans. Plants recycle oxygen. The Sun shines. The Light Wheel turns.

Sun Ray and the Sun

Sun Ray loves how the Sun makes leaves green as chlorophyll captures the sun's rays and makes food energy. Plants produce food for animals. The plants recycle oxygen.

Draw you, the Sun & the Earth

Sun Ray tells us "In nature's cycle of Photosynthesis the Sun is the Star that energized the process that eventually provides all food – proteins, carbohydrates and fats – the food all animals & humans eat. Photosynthesis also makes all the oxygen in the atmosphere for animals to breath. Of all the photosynthesis of the Earth, 2/3 takes place in the water."Sun Ray also tells us about the Sun: "You may ask how big is the sun? How far away is it from the Earth? Scientists have discovered the Sun is just one of a billion stars. It has a volume of one million times that of the Earth and is 1,392,000 kilometers in diameter. It is 150,000,000 km away from the Earth. The Sun does not rise in the morning and set in the evening. The Earth rolls and rotates on its axis as the Sun stays in one position relative to the Earth. Draw a picture of you the Sun and the Earth.

Solar Power Poster

Solar Energy is the light and heat from the Sun. It can come from changing sunlight through photovoltaic panels or mirrors to electricity. The energy created can be used to make energy for your home. Look for see solar panels on buildings or in parking lots. There is also solar thermal technology where heat from the sun is used to make hot water or steam. There is passive solar heat which is just letting the sun shine through the windows to heat the building. Solar ovens can be used to cook. Make a Solar Power Poster.

Sun Ray suggests Things to Do:

1. Use a product that uses solar energy. 2. Try to use solar panels for heat. 3. Use a solar oven. 4. Try a solar watch or calculator. 5. Thank the storekeeper for carrying products that use renewable energy like solar. 6. Show your love and gratitude for the Sun.

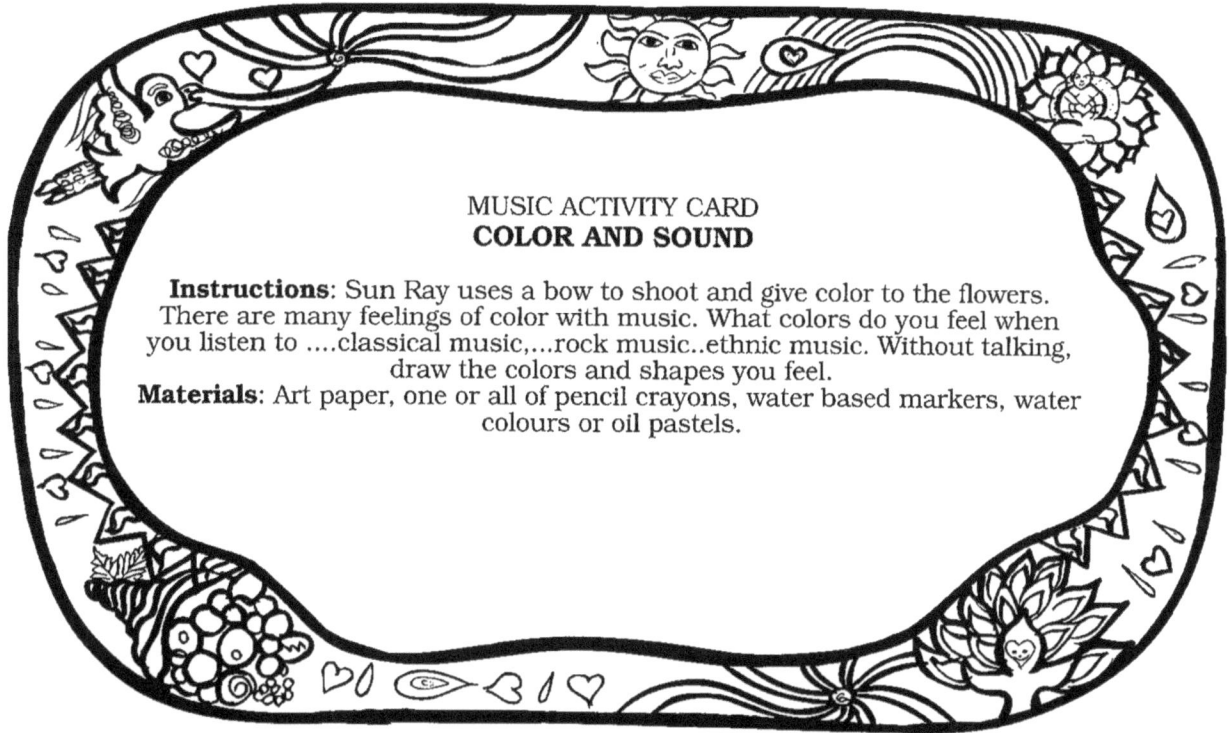

MUSIC ACTIVITY CARD
COLOR AND SOUND

Instructions: Sun Ray uses a bow to shoot and give color to the flowers. There are many feelings of color with music. What colors do you feel when you listen to ....classical music,...rock music..ethnic music. Without talking, draw the colors and shapes you feel.
Materials: Art paper, one or all of pencil crayons, water based markers, water colours or oil pastels.

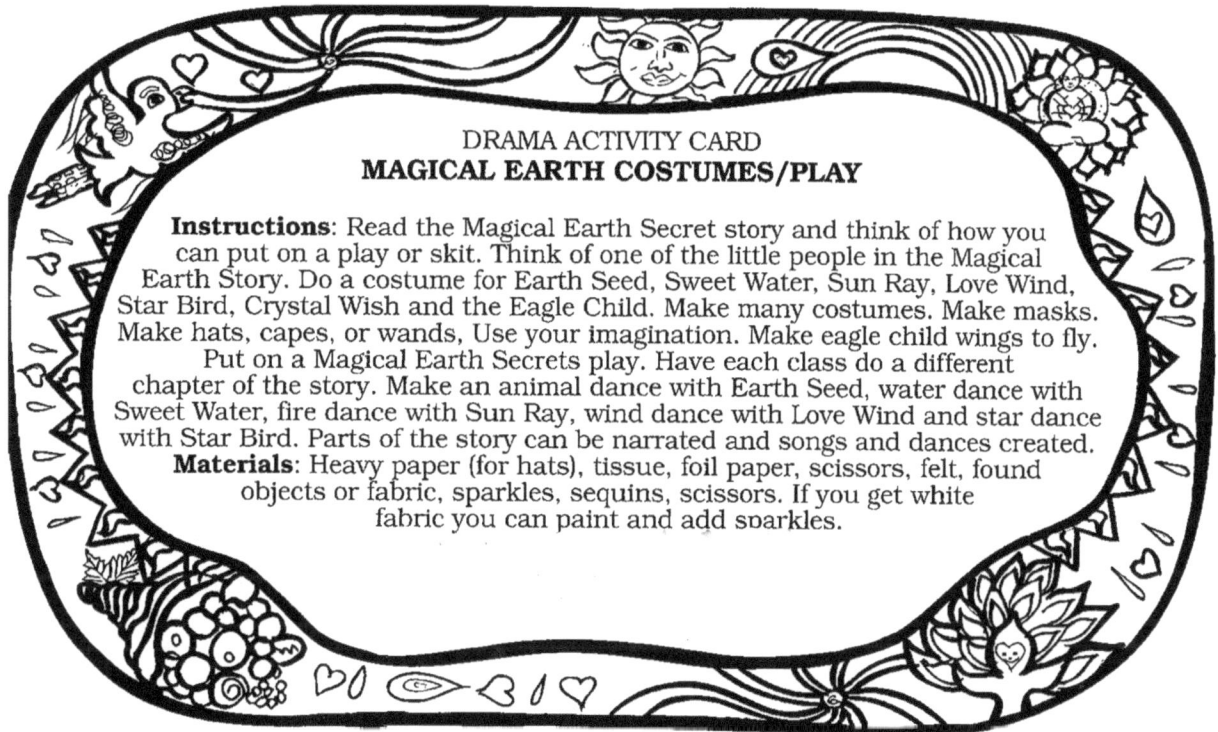

DRAMA ACTIVITY CARD
MAGICAL EARTH COSTUMES/PLAY

Instructions: Read the Magical Earth Secret story and think of how you can put on a play or skit. Think of one of the little people in the Magical Earth Story. Do a costume for Earth Seed, Sweet Water, Sun Ray, Love Wind, Star Bird, Crystal Wish and the Eagle Child. Make many costumes. Make masks. Make hats, capes, or wands, Use your imagination. Make eagle child wings to fly. Put on a Magical Earth Secrets play. Have each class do a different chapter of the story. Make an animal dance with Earth Seed, water dance with Sweet Water, fire dance with Sun Ray, wind dance with Love Wind and star dance with Star Bird. Parts of the story can be narrated and songs and dances created.
Materials: Heavy paper (for hats), tissue, foil paper, scissors, felt, found objects or fabric, sparkles, sequins, scissors. If you get white fabric you can paint and add sparkles.

'Magical Earth Secrets'- 'Magical Rainbow' in Japan
Story by Della Burford. This was produced by Kazuko
Asaba & Ruu Ruu who also designed costumes.

Dymaxium Car
by Buckminster Fuller

Buckminster Fuller invented a car called the Dymaxion. It was a most unusual shape and he told his daughter it could be called a 'zoomer' as he really wanted it to be used on land, water and even in the air.

Copies were made of the ideas but it never was produced on a large scale. It could steer in a tight circle which was very sensation. It showed at the Chicago World Fair in 1933/34.

Bucky really wanted to do more with less and designed it to use less gas. Today he ,I am sure, would use solar energy and come up with some incredible car invention using new ideas.

Dymaxion Car 1249_Richard BuckministerFuller_7dymaxioncarwikipediacommons.jpg

30 Animals that made us smarter

Draw or make a sculpture of one of the animals that made us smarter. The animals were featured and shown how they solved problems on a Podcast on BBC and now featured on the asknature.org website. What amazing creations in nature have helped us solve problems. Consider as they have on the podcast and on the website spiders doing decorations to warn the birds, geckos sticky feet, the shape of a woodpecker's beak helps high impact, the kingfisher inspired a bullet train.
https://asknature.org/collection/30-animals-that-made-us-smarter/

Fantasy Tea Party

Instructions: Solar ovens are cooas they can cook food with the sun. On a sunny day make Solar cookies that can be warmed in the sun. Also make a mint tea and heat it in the sun. Make it a sunny day celebration and draw fantasy place mats and wear your favourite Fantasy Character hats. Pretend the Smart birds, gecko, woodpecker, kingfisher and butterfly are with you. They can tell their 'smart animal' stories. The perfect Bucky setting would be either outside in nature or in a geodesic dome. If you don't have one use your imagination and picture one around you. Draw Fantasy Tea Party Art after.

Materials: Sunny Day- precooked cookie mix – unless it is really hot or you have a solar oven, tea pot, cups, Art Paper, colored pencils, markers, water colors. Elastics to use for masks.

Love wind whispered, Repeat my secret words:
"I and the air are one.
I love the air.
I will take care
of the air."

"My wings now have red, orange, yellow
and green!" shouted the Eagle Child.
"I know I can fly higher!"

THE BREATHING WHEEL

The Breathing Wheel turns. The sun makes leaves green. Leaves breath in carbon dioxide and replenish the oxygen in the atmosphere - oxygen that all animals, and humans must have in order to breath. Oxygen and food are energy. Our breath releases carcon dioxide and leaves absorb carbon dioxide in the day & oxygen at night. Daylight has come again. The birds sing. The sun makes the leaves green. Breathing Wheels turns.

What breathes in nature?

"Love the Air" Poster

Love Wind loves the Air. Love Wind says: " The Sun makes leaves green. Leaves breath in carbon dioxide and replenish with oxygen in the atmosphere. They make oxygen that all animals must have to breath. Oxygen and food are energy. Our breath releases carbon dioxide and leaves absorb it in the day ." Make a "Love the Air" Poster.

Love Wind knows to keep the air clean is essential. She knows that Pesticides, and Gases that cause Climate Change are harmful.
Love wind knows we must love the trees and plants to protect the air.
We also must understand pollution to know what is hurting our air.

Make a "Stop the Smog" Poster

Smog is the combination of factory smoke and car exhaust when they react with sunlight. Make a "Stop the Smog" Poster.

Make a "No more Pesticides" Poster

Pesticides are used to kill insects and weeds. Unfortunately, they dissolve in our soil and hurt fish, birds, and even the bees who are pollinating the food we eat. The bees also like biodiversity they do not want fields and fields of the same crop. Make a "No more Pesticides" Poster.

Make a "Stop Climate Change" Poster

This occurs when the heat from the sun is trapped unnaturally in the atmosphere. We end up having too much CO_2 in the atmosphere. When there is too much coal, oil and natural gas burnt or exhausts from too many cars or motor bikes, or when trees are slashed and burnt the atmosphere changes. During the day plants absorb CO_2. This is a natural healthy process. We must not cut down too many trees as the balance is not there. Make a "Stop Climate Change" Poster.

Love Wind's Things to Do:

1.Ride a bike, walk or share a ride. 2. Use public transport. 3. Keep cars tuned if needed to be used. 4. Use alternative sources of energy 5. Don't use sprays in your garden. 6. Plant an organic garden 7. Plant flowers for the bees and pollinators. 8. love and take care of the air.

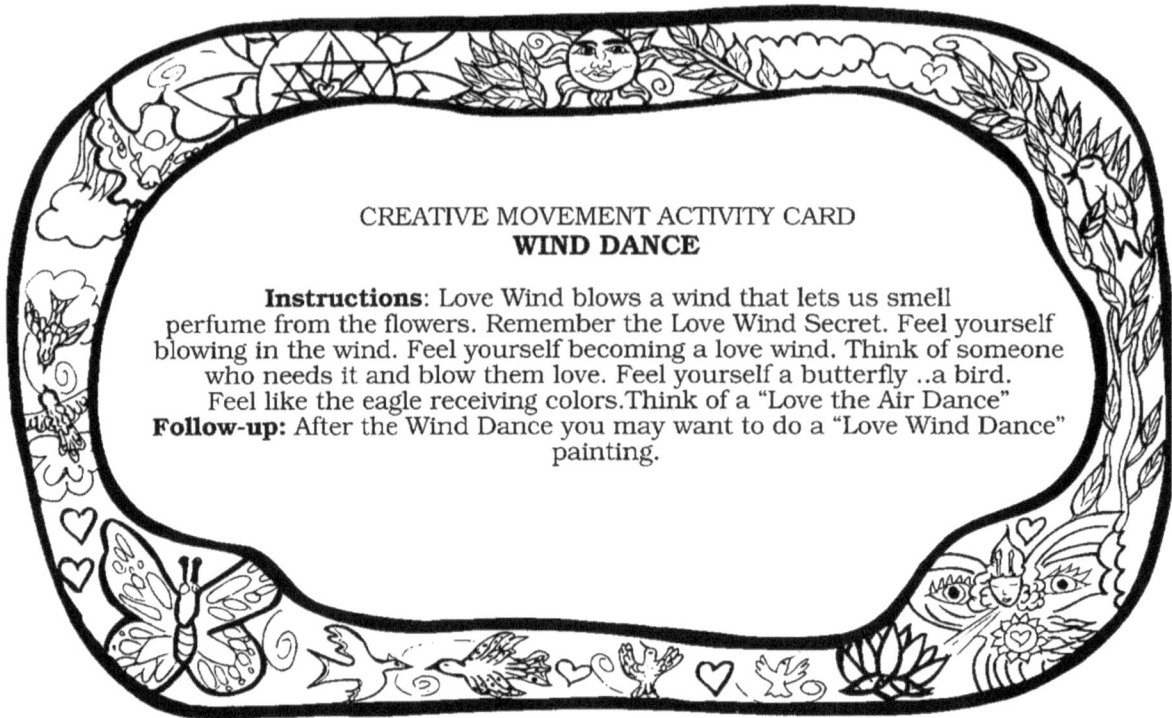

CREATIVE MOVEMENT ACTIVITY CARD
WIND DANCE

Instructions: Love Wind blows a wind that lets us smell perfume from the flowers. Remember the Love Wind Secret. Feel yourself blowing in the wind. Feel yourself becoming a love wind. Think of someone who needs it and blow them love. Feel yourself a butterfly ..a bird. Feel like the eagle receiving colors. Think of a "Love the Air Dance"
Follow-up: After the Wind Dance you may want to do a "Love Wind Dance" painting.

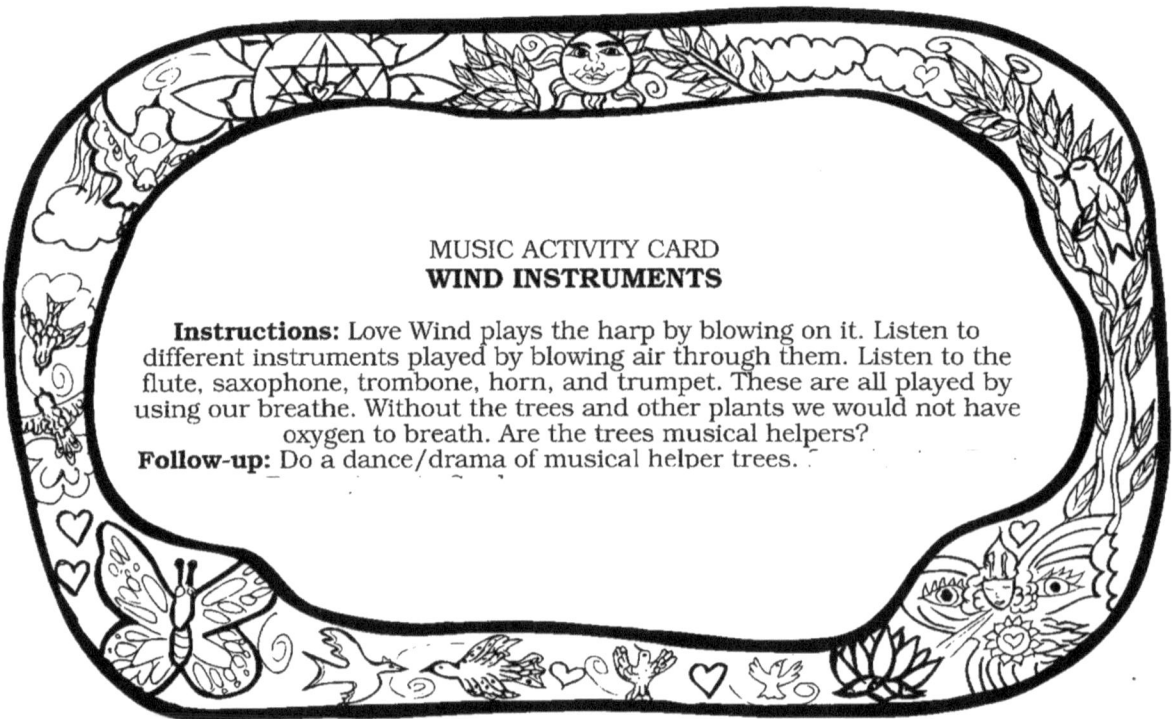

MUSIC ACTIVITY CARD
WIND INSTRUMENTS

Instructions: Love Wind plays the harp by blowing on it. Listen to different instruments played by blowing air through them. Listen to the flute, saxophone, trombone, horn, and trumpet. These are all played by using our breathe. Without the trees and other plants we would not have oxygen to breath. Are the trees musical helpers?
Follow-up: Do a dance/drama of musical helper trees.

Biosphere - Montreal

The Biosphere (French: La Biosphère), also known as the Montreal Biosphere (French: La Biosphère de Montréal), is a museum dedicated to the environment in Montreal, Quebec, Canada. It is housed in the former United States pavilion constructed for Expo 67 located within the grounds of Parc Jean-Drapeau on Saint Helen's Island. The museum's geodesic dome was designed by Buckminster Fuller. The structure was originally built for EXPO 67, which officially opened on 27 April 1967. I went and saw the Sphere at Expo and knew one day I wanted to meet Buckminster Fuller.

I saw him speak at the World Festival on Humanities in 1978 in Los Angles. To my surprise as he was speaking he became a ball of light - a mystical experience I will not forget.

Bucky and his wife first saw the dome on their 50th Anniversary. Biosphere's mission is to raise people's awareness, and promote action. One important topic is Climate Change.

Mtl_Biosphere_Montreal by Cedric Thevenet CC By-SA 3.0.jpg

One Earth - WWW.ONEEARTH.ORG/OUR-MISSION/

When Della was studying in the Space Camp of the Buckminister Fuller Institute One Earth made a presentation and she was impressed with their goals. See their goals listed in their website.

"One Earth is a nonprofit organization working to accelerate collective action to solve the climate crisis through groundbreaking science, inspiring media, and an innovative approach to climate philanthropy. The solutions for the climate crisis already exist, and the latest science led by One Earth shows we can achieve the critical 1.5°C goal through our three pillars of collective action:

A just transition to 100% renewable energy;
B.Protection and restoration of half of the world's lands and oceans;
C. shift to net-zero food and fiber systems.

The goals of the three pillars of action may sound daunting, but millions of people and organizations worldwide are already driving this transformative change. With proper resources and support, these efforts can quickly build momentum and play a critical role in solving the climate crisis in time.

One Earth's mission is
to inspire everyone to be a philanthropist for Earth, powering change from the ground up by scaling resources for and amplifying the stories of the incredible people and organizations who are actively solving the climate crisis by protecting and restoring nature and transforming our food & energy systems."

Think of a story about people or organizations solving the climate crisis by protecting and restoring nature, or transforming our food or energy systems. Della

Star Bird said:
I and the stars are one.
I love the stars.
I will take care
of the stars."

Eagle Child knew it wanted to fly to space
After seeing the Star Bird come out of
the darkness and learning the secret Eagle
Child received the power to fly to space
and got rich blue on its wings. The Star Bird
said" The stars like it when people
make wishes for the good of all."

THE ENERGY AGAIN WHEEL

The Use Again Energy Wheels turns. Renewable energy is re-NEW- able. It can be used again. Solar energy, water energy, geothermal energy, wind energy are all alternatives energy souces. They can give us heat, lights and energy to cook meals. They are powerful and renewable. We must be in gratitude.

Why must we be grateful for Renewable Energy?

Make a Renewable Energy Poster

Star Bird tells us about Alternative Energy Sources:

Fossil Fuels - Before we talk about Alternatives we have to understand what fossil fuels are. They are made of fossils. Fossils were formed over millions of years by pressure and heat on plants and tiny animals buried in the earth. Fossil fuels are considered non-renewable because when they are gone there will be no more coal, oil and gas left. They are used for energy but pollute the air and cause an in-balance.

Renewables:

Solar Energy - Using the Energy of the Sun. The sun shines on solar cells and when they are absorbed into the cells they change to electricity.

Wind Energy – The wind can be captured by wind turbines. One of the oldest forms of energy is the windmill. When the energy is captured by the wind it can be converted to mechanical and electrical energy.

Water Energy – Wave Energy – Water has an up and down movement and circular movements , with the oceans tide going in and out, water can be trapped during high tide. When it opens at low tide it can turn a turbine and this creates energy. It has to be handled with care so natural cycles ae not disturbed.

Falling Water Energy – When water falls down, the power of the movement, if trapped, can be used for electricity. This works well, but the problem is that when new dams are built, artificial lakes are formed. Dams are built to create artificial waterfalls that provide moving water just like a natural waterfall. This can disrupt the environment.

Geothermal Energy – The core of the earth is extremely hot . Some hot rocks close to the surface generate steam used in power generators.

GENI A very comprehensive study of how the different areas and even some countries of the world use renewable resources has been done by **Geni** and shown online. You can actually go into different countries and see how much renewable energy they have the option to use. What a tremendous amount of work to create this study. Think of using this link and doing a map of the different areas of the world and how much alternative energy there is in that area. This includes North America, Europe, Africa, Latin America, Asia, Oceania and the Middle East.

http://www.geni.org/globalenergy/library/renewable-energy-resources/index.shtml
http://www.geni.org/globalenergy/issues/overview/6questions-towards-peace-sustainable-development.shtml

CREATIVE MOVEMENT ACTIVITY CARD
ENERGY DIFFERENCES

Instructions: We all have energy in our bodies. Dance slowly showing how you feel when you do these three different things: when you eat something good; when you do something good for the environment; and when you think good thoughts rather than bad thoughts. It is important to put out good thoughts for yourself, others, nature and all aspects of the Earth.

ART ACTIVITY CARD
BODY ENERGY RAINBOWS

Instructions: Lie on a large piece of white paper which is cut to the length of your body and have someone else trace around you. Change the shape if you like. The first stage can be done with markers for more detail, then you can use paint. Think of the elements of nature .e.g. sun, air, water or trees. Draw different things from nature in your body. Where in you body would you show the sun, the water, the wind, trees, flowers and a rainbow. Do you see a specific animal or bird? Fill your body with colour. Show the energy around your body. What colour/pattern is it? Express you dreams and love for yourself and nature.
Materials: Large mural paper, Felt markers or oil pastels, sparkles, paint (one container for each colour of the rainbow, and some pastels plus black, white and brown).

What is loss of nature?

In my Design Science Studio class we heard Brian O'Donnell speak from Campaign for Nature campaignfornature.org

In the website the say:
"The natural world is disappearing at an unprecedented rate. The loss of nature poses a grave threat to our clean air and drinking water, the survival of wildlife, the prosperity of communities, and nature's ability to protect us.

The twin crisis of climate change and the rapid loss of biodiversity are two major problems.

Our goal is to protect at least 30% of the planet by 2030." There is now 117 countries who have pledged to protect 30%.

Dymaxion Map

This map designed by Buckminster Fuller is a projection of the World Map onto the surface of an icosahedron, which when unfolded and flattened becomes a two dimensional map of the world. With this map Bucky made the point that we are like one large island with oceans around and a 'total world'.

He developed a game called the World Peace Game in 1961 to create solutions to overpopulation and the uneven distribution of global resources. He felt the world should work for 100% humanity in the shortest time thru cooperation without damage to nature or disadvantage of anyone, thus increasing the quality of life.

A project called Geni has been done by a team of people and used his map to show the amount of enegy used in different parts of the world and how much quantity of potential solar and wind energy is possible in various countries. This can be seen on graphs online at the Geni website.

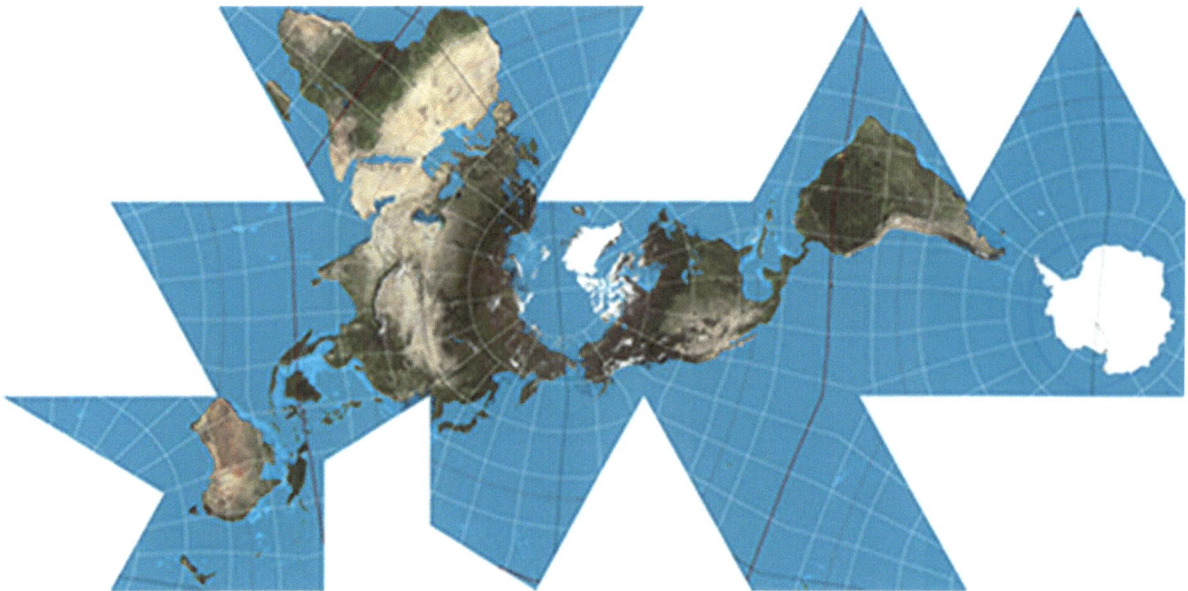

Dymaxion Projection Wikipedia Commons CCBY_SA40.png

World Energy Game Collage

Instructions:

This is like Buckminster Fuller's World Game. It works for one person or as a group activity. Choose a country and find out what you can about how energy is produced and consumed in the country. If working in a group each person chooses a different country. Do they use electrical energy in the country? Do they have the potential for solar energy, wind, geothermal, hydro or ocean energy? What's the renewable energy potential? Compare different countries in the world. Locate the countries on Bucky's Dymaxion Map which shows the countries more connected. You can put your country that you have chosen by collage and shown how much potential alternative energy it has on the map which ends of showing the potential of renewable energy in the world. Bucky designed the World Game to show we are not as separate as we think and to promote peace and look at many issues with a world view.

Materials: Art paper, mural paper, tempura paint, markers, pencil crayons.

See the Geni web page for research - link http://www.geni.org/globalenergy/issues/overview/generation-and-co2-sustainable-development.shtml

The late Dr. David Lertzman storytelling 'Magical Earth Secrets' at Earth Day in 1990. He was a role model for many students. He was Assistant Professor of Environmental Management and Sustainable Development at the Haskayne School of Business in Calgary.His work with indigenous peoples for over 20 years put him at the forefront of efforts to bridge traditional ecological knowledge and Western science in sustainable development.

When Eagle Child met
Crystal Wish
a wish was made.
"I wish the trees to grow,
the water to be clean,
the air to be fresh,
and all the people
to love and take
care of the earth."

"Because you have made such a
powerful wish
for the good of the Earth,"
Crystal Wish exclaimed. "I will give you
the color purple to complete
the full rainbow on your wings.
Imagine the full rainbow."

THE CHANGE WHEEL

The Change Wheels turns. A spark of life, an egg is formed. A caterpillar is born who weaves a cocoon from which a butterfly emerge. This is transformation. A spark of life, an egg is formed. The Change Wheel turns once again.

How do we see transformation in nature?
Buckminster Fuller quote: "There is nothing in a caterpillar that tells you it is going to be a butterfly!"

ART ACTIVITY CARD
A NATURE WISH MURAL

Instructions: Every person should make a beautiful star - draw, paint or do foil collage. Have everyone think of a wish for "the good of the earth." Put your wish for the earth in the star. Glue them all on a large mural. Paint the background.
Materials: Mural paper, art paper, one or all of a set of water-based felt markers, paint, and materials for a collage.

CREATIVE MOVEMENT ACTIVITY CARD
METAMORPHOSIS

Instructions: Show metamorphosis through movement. Show the transformation of a caterpillar to a butterfly. Show a tadpole growing into an adult frog or an environmental villain growing to be an environmental hero/heroine or helper.

Dymaxion Chronofile

The Buckminster Chronofile is a Diary of Buckminster Fuller's life. He created a scrapbook of 3 x 5 index cards containing documentation of his life every fifteen minutes for sixty three years. He included letters, sketches, and clippings from newspapers. The collection is 270 feet of paper and also includes film, audio and video. It is said to be the most important document of human life in history. He was called a logger (making a record orlogging information), but interestinglytoday we may call it blogging if shared with others.

At a low piont in his life he wondered if his life was worth living. He records that at voice came to him and reminded him he was part of the universe. After that time he made his work helping all humanity.

Dymaxion Chronofile Day Record

Instructions: As Bucky has done in his Dymaxion Chronofile make a diary of every fifteen minutes in the time period of a day FOR a day. and record in writing, what you do, who you do it with, what you eat, where you go and how you feel. You can also include drawings and photos. Share your day with others. An interesting fact is that Bucky did this for 63 years. I personally love keeping records of my dreams and have done it for 40 years I have shown this in my book 'Dream Wheels'. Today what Bucky did could be called blogging and a variation when shasred is done in personal blogs or on instagram or Facebook.

Materials: Writing paper (possibly index cards or cut paper in half), pen, pencil, pencil crayons, markers, photos (optional), (optional), video (optional)

Gumdrop Tetrahedron

Instructions: 1. Make an equilateral triangle with 9 small triangles with toothpicks and gumdrops. 2. Build tetrahedrons on each triangle.

1. 2.

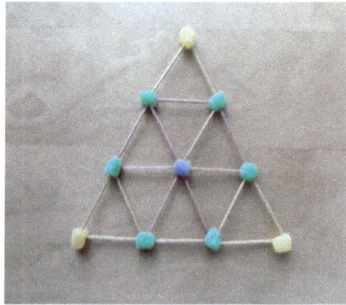

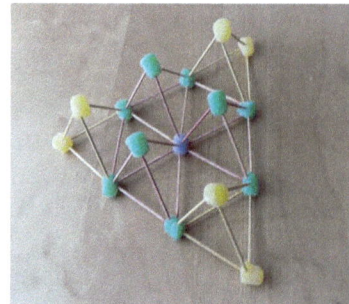

3. Connect the apex point of each tetrahedron to each other to make four equilateral traingles. Connect the top with another tetrahedron to make a 3 frequency tetrahedron.

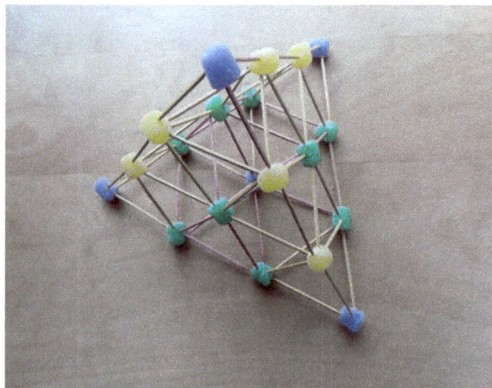

Materials: Packages of toothpicks, package of gumdrops
Activity by William Meyerhoff - based on Buckminster Fuller's
Synergetics Geometry.

Simple Geosphere

Instructions:
1. Fold plates into 6 equal triangles (like 6 pizza slices)
2.Unfold and connect plates at center to create 4 'bowties'
3. Connect opposite angle of the triangles to each other,
to create a sphere, with six square faces and eight triangular faces

1. 2.

 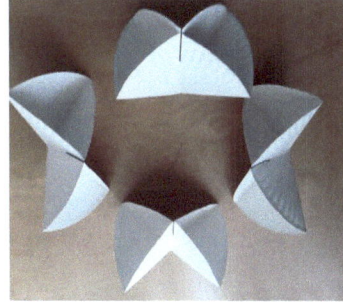

3.

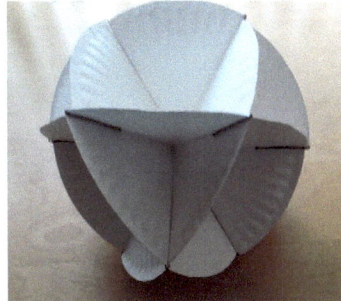 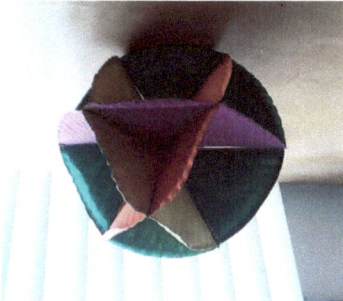

Materials: four paper plates, twelve bobby pins
To make it rainbow colored you can color the paper plates.
Activity by William Meyerhoff - based on Buckminster Fuller's
Synergetics Geometry.

Eagle child got a color from
each person of the 4 directions.
It now had the full rainbow.
Those who learned the secrets
did everything they could
to help the Earth.
Everyone made
a difference!
All is one.

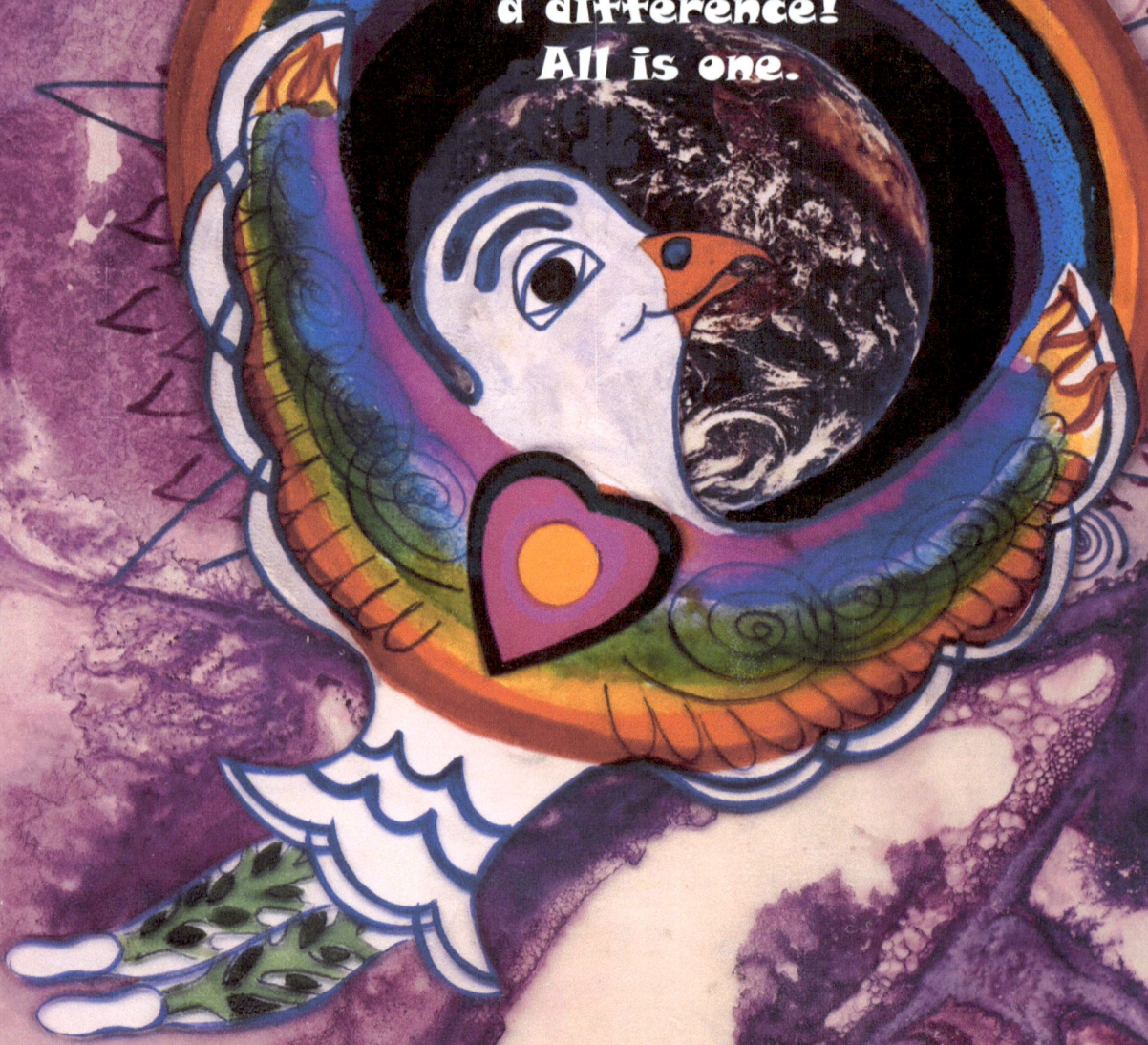

Make a Environmental Picture Book
to show your love for the Earth.

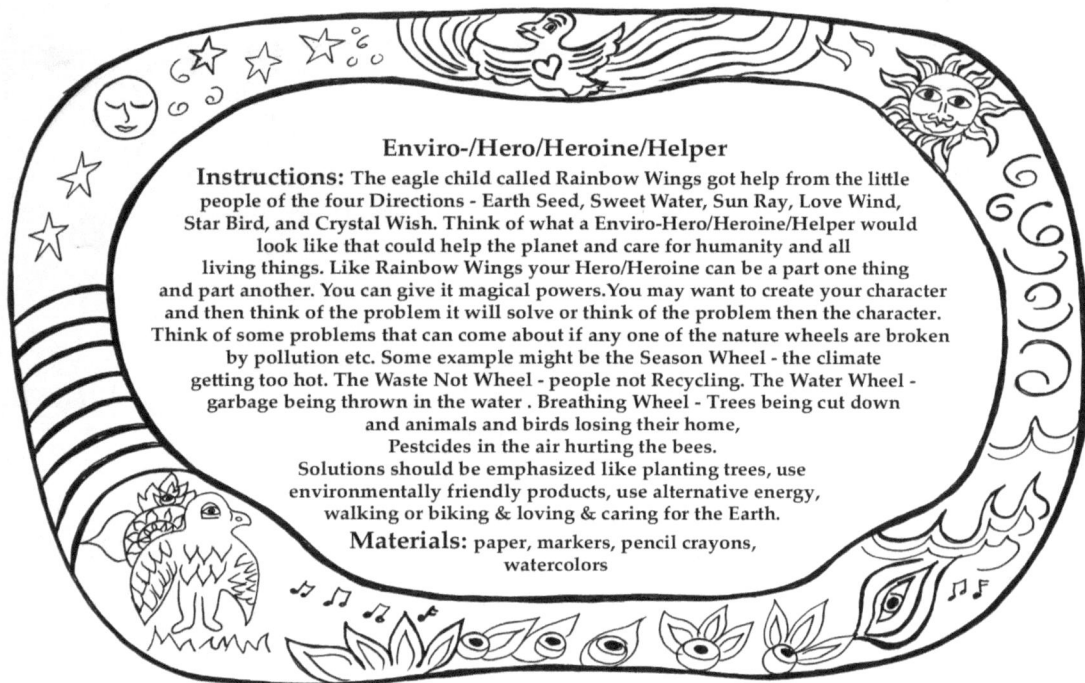

Enviro-/Hero/Heroine/Helper

Instructions: The eagle child called Rainbow Wings got help from the little people of the four Directions - Earth Seed, Sweet Water, Sun Ray, Love Wind, Star Bird, and Crystal Wish. Think of what a Enviro-Hero/Heroine/Helper would look like that could help the planet and care for humanity and all living things. Like Rainbow Wings your Hero/Heroine can be a part one thing and part another. You can give it magical powers. You may want to create your character and then think of the problem it will solve or think of the problem then the character. Think of some problems that can come about if any one of the nature wheels are broken by pollution etc. Some example might be the Season Wheel - the climate getting too hot. The Waste Not Wheel - people not Recycling. The Water Wheel - garbage being thrown in the water . Breathing Wheel - Trees being cut down and animals and birds losing their home, Pestcides in the air hurting the bees.
Solutions should be emphasized like planting trees, use environmentally friendly products, use alternative energy, walking or biking & loving & caring for the Earth.

Materials: paper, markers, pencil crayons, watercolors

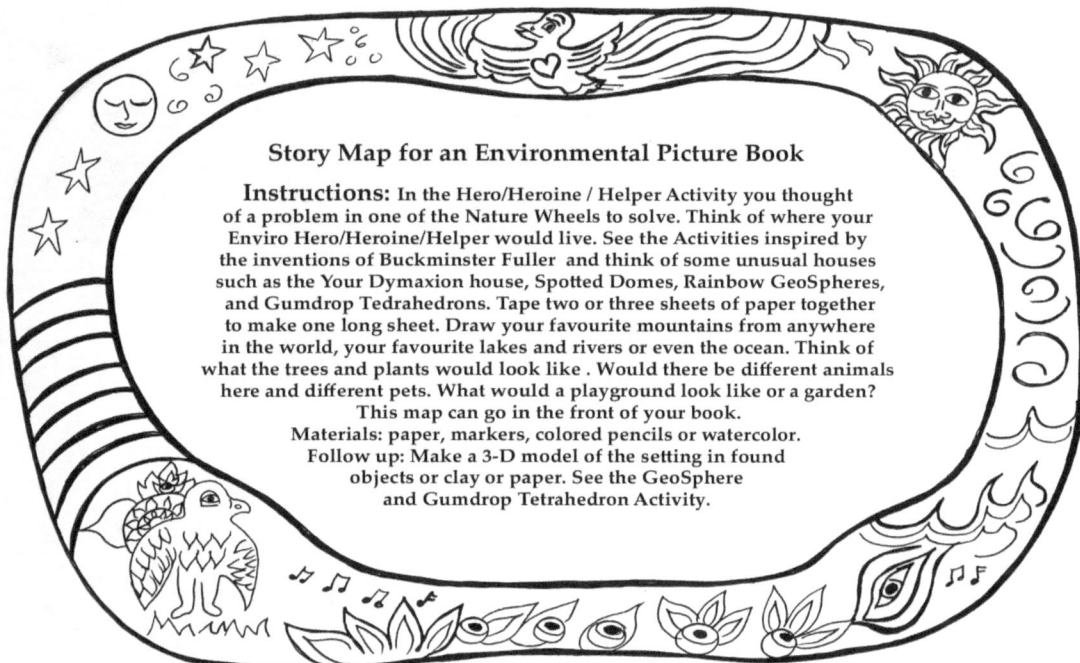

Story Map for an Environmental Picture Book

Instructions: In the Hero/Heroine / Helper Activity you thought of a problem in one of the Nature Wheels to solve. Think of where your Enviro Hero/Heroine/Helper would live. See the Activities inspired by the inventions of Buckminster Fuller and think of some unusual houses such as the Your Dymaxion house, Spotted Domes, Rainbow GeoSpheres, and Gumdrop Tedrahedrons. Tape two or three sheets of paper together to make one long sheet. Draw your favourite mountains from anywhere in the world, your favourite lakes and rivers or even the ocean. Think of what the trees and plants would look like . Would there be different animals here and different pets. What would a playground look like or a garden? This map can go in the front of your book.
Materials: paper, markers, colored pencils or watercolor.
Follow up: Make a 3-D model of the setting in found objects or clay or paper. See the GeoSphere and Gumdrop Tetrahedron Activity.

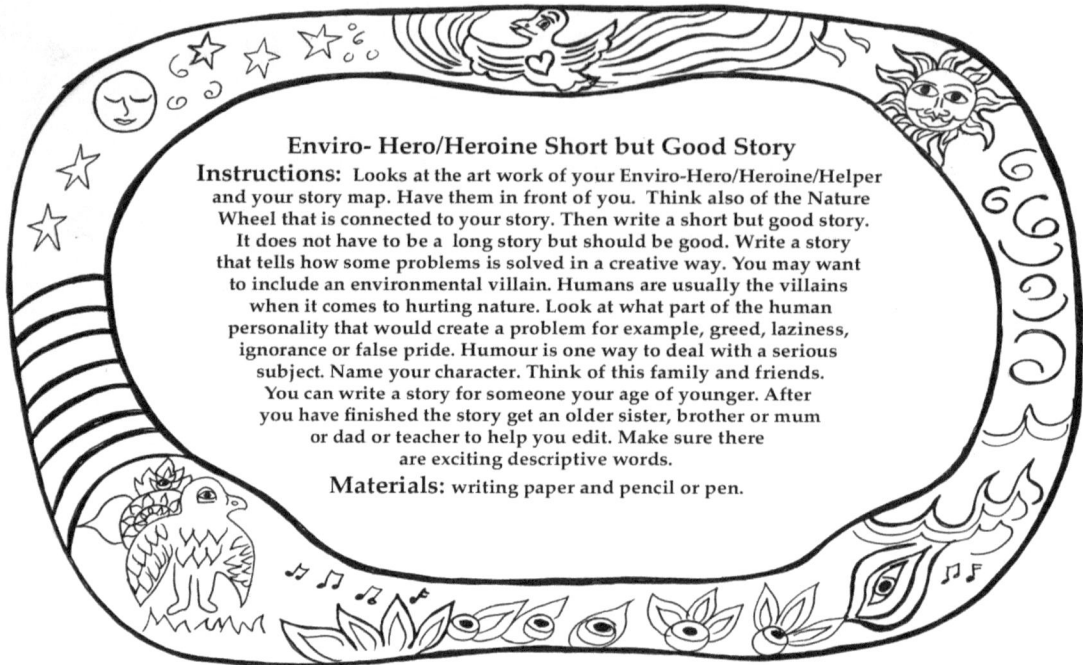

Enviro- Hero/Heroine Short but Good Story

Instructions: Looks at the art work of your Enviro-Hero/Heroine/Helper and your story map. Have them in front of you. Think also of the Nature Wheel that is connected to your story. Then write a short but good story. It does not have to be a long story but should be good. Write a story that tells how some problems is solved in a creative way. You may want to include an environmental villain. Humans are usually the villains when it comes to hurting nature. Look at what part of the human personality that would create a problem for example, greed, laziness, ignorance or false pride. Humour is one way to deal with a serious subject. Name your character. Think of this family and friends. You can write a story for someone your age of younger. After you have finished the story get an older sister, brother or mum or dad or teacher to help you edit. Make sure there are exciting descriptive words.

Materials: writing paper and pencil or pen.

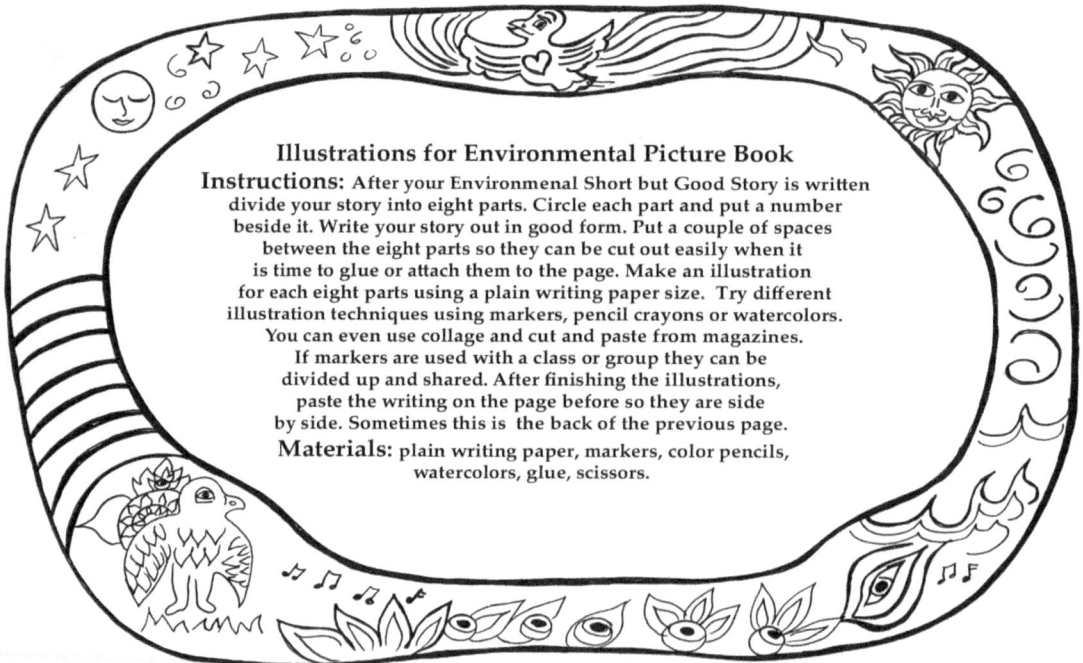

Illustrations for Environmental Picture Book

Instructions: After your Environmenal Short but Good Story is written divide your story into eight parts. Circle each part and put a number beside it. Write your story out in good form. Put a couple of spaces between the eight parts so they can be cut out easily when it is time to glue or attach them to the page. Make an illustration for each eight parts using a plain writing paper size. Try different illustration techniques using markers, pencil crayons or watercolors. You can even use collage and cut and paste from magazines. If markers are used with a class or group they can be divided up and shared. After finishing the illustrations, paste the writing on the page before so they are side by side. Sometimes this is the back of the previous page.

Materials: plain writing paper, markers, color pencils, watercolors, glue, scissors.

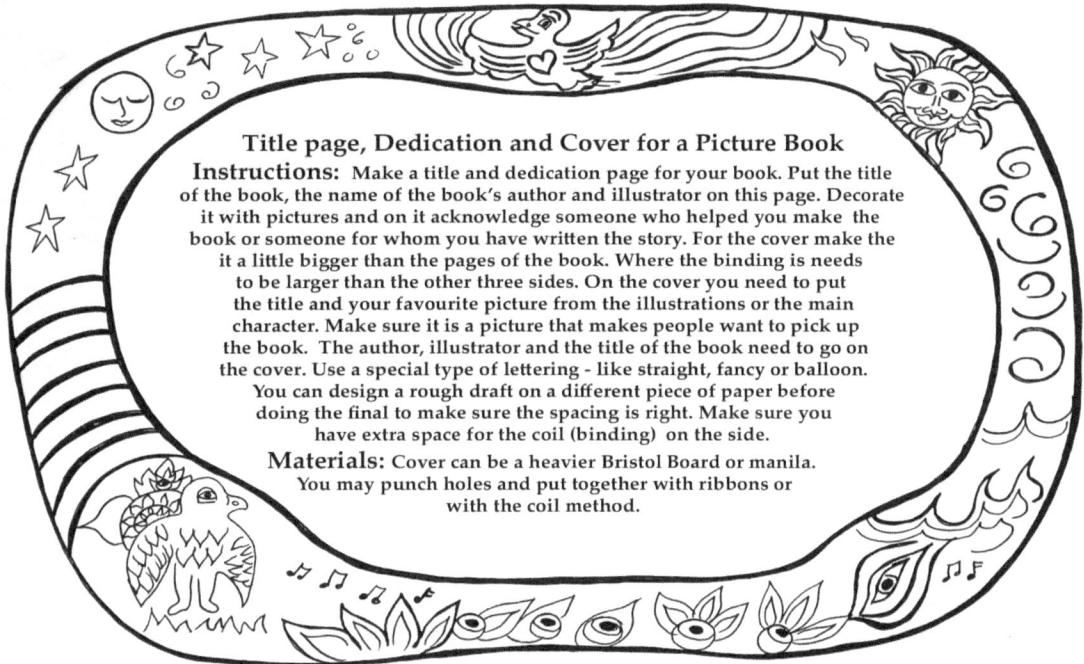

Title page, Dedication and Cover for a Picture Book

Instructions: Make a title and dedication page for your book. Put the title of the book, the name of the book's author and illustrator on this page. Decorate it with pictures and on it acknowledge someone who helped you make the book or someone for whom you have written the story. For the cover make the it a little bigger than the pages of the book. Where the binding is needs to be larger than the other three sides. On the cover you need to put the title and your favourite picture from the illustrations or the main character. Make sure it is a picture that makes people want to pick up the book. The author, illustrator and the title of the book need to go on the cover. Use a special type of lettering - like straight, fancy or balloon. You can design a rough draft on a different piece of paper before doing the final to make sure the spacing is right. Make sure you have extra space for the coil (binding) on the side.

Materials: Cover can be a heavier Bristol Board or manila. You may punch holes and put together with ribbons or with the coil method.

Enviro- Puppet Play

Instructions: After you have drawn your Enviro-Hero/Heroine/Helper you will make a puppet. You can also make a puppet of some of the little people of the Four Directions - Earth Seed, Sweet Water, Sun Ray, Love Wind, Star Bird or Crystal Wish. When you draw your Hero/Heroine/Helper or them - draw them large enough to fill a page. Now you can make this as a pattern for a stick puppet. Put paper on top and trace around it to make a pattern. Cut this out for your pattern. Lay this pattern on a peice of felt. Lay it near the corners so the felt material is not wasted. Trace around with a crayon or chalk to see it. Cut out all pieces. Cut out cardboard for the back.The cardboard has to be heavy enough to hold the puppet up. Glue a flat stick between he cardboard and fabric. Make a Puppet Theatre looking at setting from your Story Map. You may draw a large setting to paste on the back of the Theatre or or make 3-D figure if you have GeoSpheres (to hang) , Gumdrop Tetrahedrons, Spot Domes or Dymaxium Houses, etc. in your story. Work with another person to make a play. Through the telling of the story you will come up with a creative solution.

Materials: Art paper, markers, colored penxils, felt, glue, cardboard,glue, scissors, flat sick to put on the back of the puppet

Song for Eagle Child & Earth Seed, Sweetwater, Sun Ray, Love Wind, Star Bird & Crystal Wish.

The Season Wheel connected to the Waste-Not Wheel.
The Waste-Not Wheel connected to the Food Chain Wheel.
The Food Chain Wheel connected to the Water Wheel.
The Water Wheel connected to the Light Wheel.
The Light Wheel connected to the Breathing Wheel.
The Breathing Wheels connected to the Energy Again Wheel
The Energy Again Wheels connect to Change Wheel.
The Change Wheel connected to the Season Wheel
Oh Dear Mother Earth
The Earth, The Earth, Mother Dear Earth
The Earth, The Earth, Mother Dear Earth
All Wheels connected - All is One.
Oh Dear Mother Earth

Eagle Child Hat - Wear the Eagle Hat to feel your power to love and protect the earth. Color the colors you love. Can enlarge or glue on heavier paper. Attach a band.

Fly like the eagle!

Design Science Studio

Della was pleased to be part of **Co-heart 2** and now **Co-heart 3**
From the Design Science website we read:
We are in a time of radical systems change. **It is time to align humanity with Nature** AS Nature once again. It's time to reimagine everything: From eco-systems, to thinking toolkits, from new governance systems, to eco-village blueprints…New regenerative practices, protest music, protopian design, inspiring art and experiences…
We are birthing the Regenaissance.

We are the creators: fine artists, designers, performers, philosophers, ecologists, systems thinkers and others who resonate with this prompt to create art that explores the **principles of Design Science**.

Buckminster Fuller was inspired by nature, and we currently know more about living systems than we ever have. Whether you are visualizing what society aligned with the principles of nature will look l ike or creating technology that will help us get there, we invite you to join our community of collaborators. **Through creative expression, members of this program will co-create in service of a world that works "for 100% of humanity in the shortest possible time, through spontaneous cooperation, without ecological offense or the disadvantage of anyone"**.

 The Design Science Studio has a new group of Evolutionary artist – coheART3 who are applying their whole system to create evolutionary Art, experiences and messages for a regenerative future for ALL LIFE.
See the link to the **CohART 3** below:
https://www.designscience.studio/revolutionaries2023
Meet the Artist of **CohART 1**
https://www.designscience.studio/revolutionaries2020
Meet the Artists of **CohART 2**
https://www.designscience.studio/revolutionaries2021

Magical Earth Secrets is danced in the story and has been danced in New York, Edmonton, Japan and Bali. Also in school performances.

Earth Dance

Water Dance

Sun Dance

Star Dance

Magical Earth Secrets New York

Magical Earth Secrets Bali

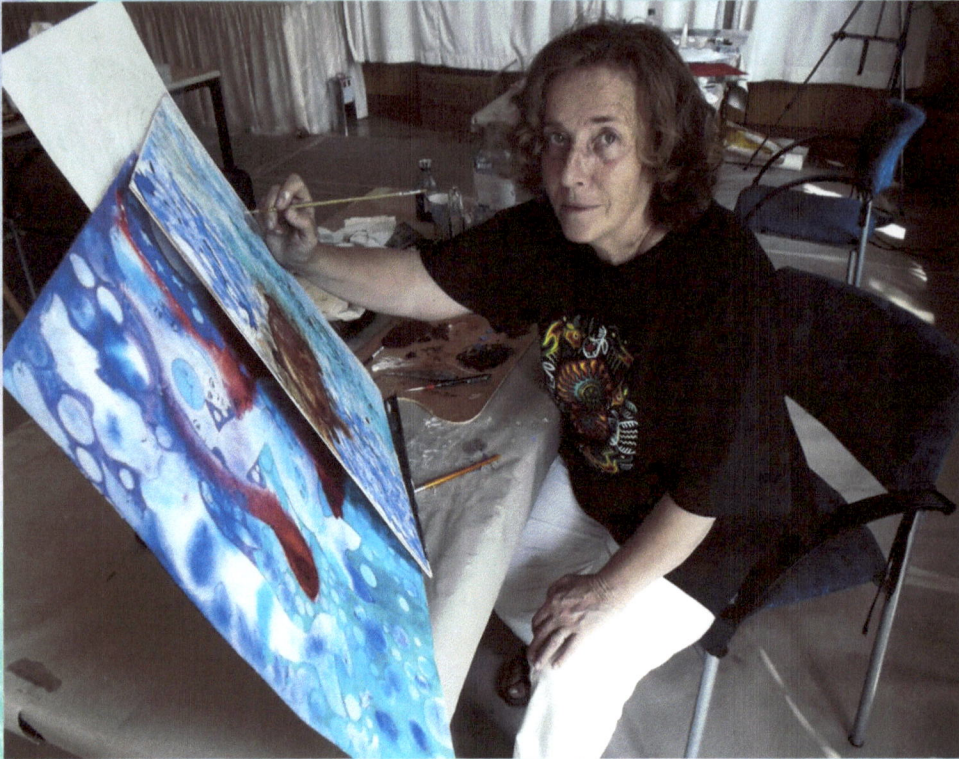

DELLA BURFORD is a Canadian artist/author based on Vancouver Island. She studied the Interior Design at N.Y.S.I.D., Textiles at U. of A. , Education in the Artist in the Community B.Ed. program at Queen's University . She learned Mischtechnik of the Flemish and Italian Renaissance painters in Vienna. She taught Interior Design for six years at Humber College. Her first book published (writing and art) in 1977 Journey to Dodoland won a P.I.A. Award for design.

Della won first in Graphic Art for her painting 'Shaman's Eye' in the Visionary Art Show in Moscow. She has shown her painting in Toronto & Bali and with the Society for Art of Imagination in Ottawa, Montreal, New York , Peru and London England. She has facilitated workshops around her books in N.Y.C., Canada thru Inner City Angels, Ontario Art Council and Canada Council, Also shared in Gautemala, Mexico, Sweden, Holland, England, Korea, Japan & Bali.

Journey to Dodoland was chosen to launch the government sponsored program Swiftsure and became an e-zine and website that has had 2 million people visit.

Her book "Magical Earth Secrets" was a best-seller in Canada. It has been a play in New York, Edmonton and Japan. Her work is encouraging other to be creative, to take action to help the earth, and make a difference in the World. She loves collaborating and in doing a Trimtab Space Camp - Design Science Redux program with the Buckminster Fuller Institute in 2021 did the final edit of 'Earth Action'. She is very grateful for all who have helped take this work to the world. Her work is for self-development, Humanity, and the World.

DALE BERTRAND was born in Prince Rupert, B.C. and raised in California and
western Canada. He studied photography at "Three Small Schools", Toronto and
desk top publishing at Ryerson. He has photographed in Wales, Japan, India, Hawaii,
Guatemala, Peru, Thailand, Mexico and Bali.

  He was Communication Manager for the Harbourfront Antique Market for eight
years. Dale has had various art shows of the Early Canadian artist Tomhu Huron
Roberts and produced 6 book on his father John Hugh Roberts mystical Celtic writing.

   Dale did some background paintings for Magical Earth Secrets and co- authored
 the original Activity cards. In 'Journey to Dodoland' he created Giant Flower Islands.
He participated in the Guatemala production of Dodoland and in the storyelling of
Magical Earth Secrets in Korea. He joined Della in Japan to see 'Magical Rainbow'.

   Dale has co- designed with Della the Dodoland in Cyberspace website that was
created in 1995 as a children e-zine It has had 2 million visitors.

   Dale has led many workshops such at Medicine Wheels & Art Murals with
Inner City Angel and Environmental Posters in the Nanaimo Art Gallery Program.
His canvases done with children were taken to the Future Meeting in Stockholm.
He has also shared 'Druidical Quest' in workshops in both Holland and Bali.

   Dale has taught English (1 year) in Mexico doing start up for a Canadian
school. He also taught 10 yrs Communications & Business at an English school in
Vancouver. He is presently a Caregiver for indigenous youth in the Vancouver area
 as well as keeping his love of beads and antiquities hobby going.

Thanks so much!

Thanks so much to all the people at the **Canada Network for Arts and Learning** for their programs in helping me make the shift to more online participation. Thanks to the **Buckminster Fuller Institute** and their **Trimtab Space Camp Design Science Redux Program** where I was able to to lead a Mission to edit the 'Earth Action' book

Thanks to **Faith Flanigan**, **Jazmine Cable** , and **Amber Joy Ravenhill** who led programs/ zoom sessions at the Buckminster Fuller Institute. Participants in this program - I want to thank **William Meyerhoff** who joined me to brainstorm the Bucky activities. Being an architect and having knowledge of Bucky and educational experience in programs with children has and will enhance the project. Thanks also to **Peter Meisen** who gave me Renewable Energy advice and turned me on to the **Geni** website which uses the Bucky's World Map to show Energy usage in the world and goes into other important aspects of his philosophy. Also thanks to **Erin** who shared using ideas on using a Solar Oven, and **Kassandra Huynh** who shared being in touch with nature and Biomimicry. I am thankful to the "Office Hour" programs and found **Tom Chi** talk on Rapid Prototyping inspiring for the first edit of the book and began to visualize it more clearly and trimmed it to half the length.

I am also thankful to **Janine Benyus** who shared her ideas in a talk and also on the Biomimicry website **Asknature** website. **Barbera Wall** who shared her indigenous wisdom and **Mickey McManus** for white board ideas.

I am also thankful to **Jacquie Howardson** for editing.
Always thankful to **Dale Bertrand** for his original Activity Ideas and brain storming, and developing new ideas. Rosemary Scherba for her help.
Thanks to **Western Canada Wilderness Committee** and the original vision of **Paul George, Adrian Carr** , **Elaine Jones**, **Sue Fox** to create the book "Magical Earth Secrets". Thanks to **Dr. David Lertzman** for storytelling.
Thanks to the Directors of the **Earth Child Foundation** – Dale Bertrand, **Tom Williams, Mary Lynne Ogilvie, Julia Atkins and Edna Ret**i – (Sal &Doug)
Thanks to the **Inner City Angels** who organized many workshops .
Thanks to **Tedrian Chizik, Merian Soto, Mirabel Daniels, Diane Godynick** for the New York Production of Magical Earth Secrets.
Thanks to David Walsh for help in many projects.
Thanks to Barney Williams for contributing to the publication of the 1st Edition.
Thanks to **Maria Formolo, Noreen Crone Findlay** - Edmonton Production.
Thanks to **Paul Vrenken** for the video of "Magical Earth Secrets" in Holland and **Marijke Sluijter** for the translation to Dutch
Thanks to **Kazuko Asaba & Ruu Ruu** for 'Magical Earth in Japan.
Thanks to **I Made Sidia and Paripurna Dance** for 'Magical Earth in Bali.
Thanks to all family - Burford & Williams and friends. Della Burford

www.ingramcontent.com/pod-product-compliance
Lightning Source LLC
Chambersburg PA
CBHW060859270326
41935CB00003B/31